Successful **Motivation**
in a week

Successful
Motivation
in a week

CHRISTINE HARVEY

Hodder & Stoughton

A MEMBER OF THE HODDER HEADLINE GROUP

Orders: please contact Bookpoint Ltd, 39 Milton Park, Abingdon, Oxon OX14 4TD. Telephone: (44) 01235 400414, Fax: (44) 01235 400454. Lines are open from 9.00 - 6.00, Monday to Saturday, with a 24 hour message answering service. Email address: orders@bookpoint.co.uk

British Library Cataloguing in Publication Data

Harvey, Christine
  Successful Motivation in a Week. –
  (Successful Business in a Week Series)
  I. Title   II. Series
  650.1

ISBN 0 340 73761 1

First published 1992
Second edition 1998
Impression number   10 9 8 7 6 5 4 3 2 1
Year   2004 2003 2002 2001 2000 1998

Typeset by Multiplex Techniques Ltd, St Mary Cray, Kent.
Printed in Great Britain for Hodder & Stoughton Educational, a division of Hodder Headline Plc, 338 Euston Road, London NW1 3BH by Cox & Wyman Ltd, Reading, Berkshire.

the Institute
of Management

FOUNDATION

The Institute of Management (IM) exists to promote the development, exercise and recognition of professional management. The Institute embraces all levels of management from student to chief executive and supports its own Foundation which provides a unique portfolio of services for all managers, enabling them to develop skills and achieve management excellence.

For information on the various levels and benefits of membership, please write to:

Department HS
Institute of Management
Cottingham Road
Corby
Northants NN17 1TT
Tel. 01536 204222

This series is commissioned by the Institute of Management Foundation.

C O N T E N T S

Introduction		8
Sunday	The morale building process	9
Monday	The power to change	21
Tuesday	The confidence building process	35
Wednesday	The three part reinforcement process	47
Thursday	The dolphin process	63
Friday	The anti-procrastination process	76
Saturday	The goal focus process	84
	The week in summary	95

Christine Harvey is a businesswoman and author of five best selling motivational books for self development, published in 20 languages:

- *Secrets of the World's Top Sales Performers*, 150,000 copies sold
- *Successful Motivation in a Week*, 13 languages
- *Successful Selling in a Week*, 12 languages
- *In Pursuit of Profit*, 140,000 copies sold, and
- *Power Talk – Public Speaking and Leadership*, 6 languages

Mrs. Harvey gives freely of her time to address service organisations and is in demand worldwide to address corporate audiences with success stories to help them achieve their goals.

Many of her books and tapes have been turned into TV and radio series. In addition to running her own training and consulting company, Intrinsic Marketing, in West Drayton, Middx, she serves on the Board of Adler Geneva Financial Corporation, is on the Council of the National Speakers Association, is a Toastmaster and Toastmaster Club Sponsor, is Past Director of Zonta International, and past west section Chairman of the London Chamber of Commerce.

Her Motivation Seminars for the public and for corporations are offered through the Institute of Management.

Motivation is a commodity everyone wants more of. We need it on a daily basis to run our lives, to help others, to lead people and to reach our goals.

The ability to motivate ourselves and others affects our success in business and our satisfaction in life. By using a few practical methods, we can improve our results enormously.

Mastering one method each day of the week
The steps are:
- Achieving your goals
- Gaining a positive perspective
- Creating the power to change
- Building self-esteem
- Reinforcing desired performance
- Moving from weakness to strength
- Stop procrastination

Remember that motivation can be the most rewarding of skills and is achievable by everyone. There is no limit to the situations in which it can be applied, or to the level of expertise you can reach.

The morale building process

Research shows that attitude is 10% determined by outside forces and 90% determined by our own minds. If this is true, why then is our attitude to life so often different from what we want it to be?

Part of the reason is that we model our attitude from people around us at such an early age that we don't ask ourselves if that's the attitude we want for life.

No wonder we struggle with it and feel it doesn't fit us. In fact, it doesn't. It fits like someone else's shoe.

The attitude that motivates

What shoes would fit better? If we look at the most motivated people, we find that they have three attitudes which guide their life perspective. These are:

- Positivity
- Gratitude
- Self-worth

Let's examine the first.

Positivity

Imagine for the moment that you are standing at the edge of a pond. Imagine that in your hands you hold two pebbles. In your left hand you hold a pollution pebble and if you throw that one in the pond, it will *pollute* the water for generations to come.

In your right hand you hold a purification pebble, and if you throw that one in the pond it will *purify* the water for generations to come. The choice of which pebble to throw is yours.

Now imagine for a moment that the words we use are like the pebbles and the water is like the people in our lives. If we choose negative words, they pollute our mind and they *destroy* motivation of ourselves, of other people and, perhaps, of generations to come.

If we choose positive words, on the other hand, we purify, we support, we motivate.

What kind of environment can you create with your words for yourself and for the people in your life?

Don't pollute your motivation
Can you afford to be more gentle with yourself? Less hard on yourself? People often have wonderful achievements and talents and yet they choose to belittle themselves by focusing on what they didn't achieve or can't do. Is this honouring the true potential we have within us? Is this purifying or polluting our motivation?

Can you afford to be more positive with other people? A man came up to me after a speech I made and said, 'I'm going home with a completely new approach to my son. He's been trying to start a business and I've been telling him everything I thought he was doing wrong. I thought I was helping. Now I'm going to point out all the positive things he's doing and build up his faith.'

He realised that the ripple effect, like the pebble in the water, would carry his motivation from person to person and back again into their relationship.

What about your life? Who is waiting for *you* to motivate *them*? Think of your career. Think of your family. Think also of your associations. What can you say to people in order to let them see their successes – to keep them going?

We do it automatically with children. When they learn to walk, we cheer them on. We clap. We give them words of encouragement. We don't wait until they fall down and then say, 'Stupid'. Yet that's often what happens in business and the community. We criticise people the minute something goes wrong, but we forget to give them positive reinforcement to keep them going.

As one plaque at the registration table of a social club reads, 'Don't criticise others for the way things are being done unless you're prepared to volunteer to do it yourself'.

No wonder we don't get as much support from members of the community and employees as we would like and that often we lose them altogether. The minute they do something, someone criticises. And who balances it with positive feedback? Very few, or no one. Yet, who could give

positive reinforcement? You could start to think of yourself
as a motivator. Realise that you may be the *only* one in that
person's life who is able to give positive reinforcement.

Be conscious of your power
Think again of those purification and pollution pebbles.
What can you commit to doing to purify the waters of the
mind? Your mind and the minds of others?

Gratitude

One saying which Mr Carnegie, the legendary motivator,
asks people to consider is this:

> *Two men looked out through prison
> bars. One saw the mud, the other the
> stars.*

We have the power to see the best or the worst of every
situation. The mud and the stars are both there. It's our
choice which we focus on. When we focus on the mud, we
feel bogged down. When we focus on the stars, we feel hope
and gratitude.

Think for a moment of the world around us. In the 1990s,
millions of people became free of the Communist system.
For them, despite the economic struggles, the pleasures of
freedom and openness in society are marvellous. These are
pleasures we take for granted.

Each time I travel to and from the ex-Eastern bloc,
I experience culture shock in each direction. On entering,
I have the realisation that these are people with whom we

share a common heritage, and yet they have so little of the luxury we take for granted.

And on leaving and re-entering my own environment, I have the feeling of imbalance for having so much which we seldom appreciate; well-paved roads, telephones that work, goods in the shops.

Think of all the things we have to be grateful for. The marvel of our creation. The power of our brain to create, of our heart and our soul to love and to feel. And yet, how much do we value them?

We're not even behind prison bars, and yet we don't let ourselves see the stars.

When we focus on gratitude, there's no room for negativity. When we focus on gratitude, motivation automatically comes through. Gratitude, in fact, blocks out negativity.

One of the most successful and self-motivated people I know has this three-step thought process for going to sleep at night. Her name is Hilde Bartlett and she was honoured with the Taylor Woodrow 'Women in Business Award' at Downing Street. Try it and see what results *you* get.

1. *Who* do I have to be grateful for today?
2. *What* do I have to be grateful for today?
3. *What* are my hopes and goals for tomorrow?

Gratitude, like positivity, is contagious and magnetic. If we want to motivate others, let's start with ourselves, then go foward.

Self-worth

It's easy to see how self-worth is important to our own motivation, but let's look first at how important it is in motivating other people at work and in the community. If you want more cooperation from the people around you, try this.

Use self-worth as a motivator
Two executives in London were faced with the fact that their service club was flagging in membership and they had to do something quickly or it would face collapse. They planned their strategy for gaining new members and decided to put their first focus on giving attention to their current members.

Here's what they did. They put a table at the door of the meeting room with two of their most friendly committee members. Then they greeted each member as they entered, and poured them a glass of wine. Next, they got them engaged in conversation with another member. In other words, they showed them that they mattered.

They also sent out a newsletter a few days before each meeting announcing the speaker. They had a telephone committee who called each member personally three days before the meeting to say they looked forward to seeing them. Notice they said 'looked forward to seeing them.' That's different from pressuring them or making them feel guilty; it's making them feel important.

The attendance by members shot up immediately. And they kept coming. They brought friends. The membership grew just by taking care of the old members.

People need to feel wanted and cared about. Their self-worth is important and it's up to us to enhance it. When each person's self-worth is high, the group's morale is high. When the group's morale is high, the group flourishes.

Self-worth transference to organisations
Have you ever stopped to listen to some people about their company? It sometimes seems that they can find nothing good to say about it. Yet the company might have a 50 year history of serving the community and be recognised for good quality.

Why should this be so? Well, if a person's feeling of self-worth is low, they transpose that image on to their organisation.

We should consider it our responsibility to help them see the best in themselves. Gradually, as their self-esteem goes up, they'll begin to see the best in their company.

Self-worth acknowledgement for yourself
One secondary school teacher in America gave his students the assignment of writing an autobiography. Included in it,

he told them, must be a statement about the student's strengths and talents.

Upon getting this assignment, most of the students were dumbfounded. No one could say anything good about themselves. It didn't seem right to them.

Finally one of the students went to the teacher to admit his dilemma. This is what he reports hearing the teacher say. 'You know Terry, the problem with our upbringing is that we're taught to be so modest that we don't even see the value in ourselves. It doesn't help us to serve the purpose we were put here for. It doesn't help us fulfil the reasons for our existence.'

Terry was only 14 when he had that experience, and the impact was great. He developed an attitude he uses in management today. The attitude is this:

'It's all right to honour our own humanity and to honour the humanity of others. It's all right to honour our organisation and all that we work for. It's all right for all of us to help others to learn that too.'

Realisation about motivation

What realisation do we come to about motivation from
people who succeed best as motivators?

First, we must be positive, not negative. When we are
positive we draw people to us like a magnet. When we
are positive with other people, we feel good about
ourselves.

Second, we must have gratitude. When we do, we
project harmony which is rare and attractive in group
dynamics. It draws the best people to us.

Third, we should never underestimate the importance
of self-worth for without it, we cannot fulfil our potential.

Each of us has phenomenal ability. Each of us has been
given phenomenal talent. When it comes to motivation, it's
easy to think that our life can change from gaining new
information. But is information or knowledge alone enough?

Will it do us any good, for example, to know that people need positive words of encouragement from us, if we don't provide them? Is it enough to understand that we *can* affect the self-esteem of others, if we don't *do* it?

No. Knowledge without action creates no change. It's like standing at the edge of the pond with those purification pebbles in your hand, but not using them. It's having the power, but not using it. It does no good for anyone.

Think carefully of the impact of your positivity, your gratitude and your self-worth on yourself and on the people in your life. Take today to decide what specific actions you will take.

Actions You Will Take

Positivity

....
....
....

Gratitude

....
....
....

Self-worth

....
....
....

Motivation Action Sheet

Use the action section below to enhance your own techniques and achievements.

Ideas for development:

1 Examine the words you use in speaking and writing. What percentage are negative and what percentage are positive?

2 Decide if you belittle yourself unnecessarily.

3 See if you criticise people with your comments, jokes or questions.

4 Remind yourself regularly of the power of your words and thoughts.

5 Decide if gratitude plays a large enough part in your life.

6 Is your self-worth high enough? If not, list your strengths and stop thinking about your weaknesses.

7 Other points as they relate to you (complete according to your needs).

Answers
- Of the above ideas, which one is likely to yield the best results for you?
- What percentage performance increase could realistically be expected?
- How long would it take:
  - to develop the idea?
  - to get results?
- Who would have to be involved?
- What date should you start?
- What is the first step you should take?

The power to change

The power of the mind to help us reach our goal is enormous. It's there, we need only to use it. The following true story will give you insight into the power we have available.

A woman I know from Thailand had been on holiday in the Yugoslav mountains and was resting in her car parked on the cliff's edge while her companions were hiking.

She was in the back seat when she noticed that the hand brake was not set, and leaned forward to secure it. At that moment, the shift of weight in the small car caused it to roll forward and within a few seconds she was tumbling down the cliff to what she was sure would be death by drowning in the sea far below.

As she rolled over and over, the car banged against the rocks. Her life passed in front of her and she knew that death was near. There seemed to be no escape.

Suddenly, amidst the turmoil, she remembered her deep belief that *we have the power within us to change any situation*. Could it be applied to this, she wondered? Then she focused every fragment of energy she had left to see if there were any changes she could make in her situation. All the while the car continued to crash down the cliff.

The instant she focused on change, her mind brought forward an idea. If she were able to open the door and put her foot out to keep it open, then when the car hit the water she could escape from it. She tried and after several very difficult attempts, she managed to do it.

Miraculously she escaped death. After eight long months of hospitalisation, she had her life back in order again. She is certain that without her change in focus, deciding that she had the power to change the situation, she would be dead.

Consider her last words as you read them again because they are the decisive words:

> 'She *decided* she had the power to change the situation.'

Most of us are not tumbling off cliffs to our death. The crises we face are mundane by comparison, but the power within us to change our situation is the same.

Take time to think for a moment of what changes you want to create.

The Thai woman decided on an action which was different from her previous action. That was opening the door, despite heavy resistance from tumbling and turning, and putting her foot out for a brace with the risk of losing it to save her life.

In the mundane events of life, we often do the opposite. We give away our life to save our foot. The things that we really want, we sacrifice. We give away the treasures of life, and the possibility of finding our real potential, for the sake of staying in our comfort zone.

Reverse 'limitation' thinking

What would you do if you knew you couldn't fail at anything? Studies show that 'limitation' thinking about ourselves comes into play between six and 12 years of age. If you ask children at age six if they think they can succeed at something, 90% say yes. At the age of 12, only 10% say yes.

Here's a process that can put you in touch with what your visions in life were before they were tarnished with limitation thinking and road blocks.

Just clear your mind for a moment, and imagine a fantasy in which your fairy godmother has told you that you can be anything you want. *Anything*. She's told you not to worry about limitations of money. Don't worry about education or any other limitation. You can be *anything* you want. Trust her, she says. She will make it all possible.

Imagine now, waking up in the morning as the ideal you. What qualities do you have?

Imagine the room you wake up in. See the light coming in. See the colours, see the size of the room, see how it's decorated. Listen for the sounds inside and outside.

Now see yourself sitting up in bed and putting your feet on the floor. What do you feel? Carpet, wood, tiles or what?

See yourself getting up and walking to your wardrobe, knowing that when you open it you'll see all the clothes that you really want for your perfect, ideal life. Now open it. What do you see? How do you feel about yourself?

Imagine that this is a week day and that you are getting ready to do exactly the kind of work you want to do.

You choose the clothes for it and get ready to go. As you leave the house, you look around you. Where are you? Are you in the country or the city? Do you see trees? Do you see streets, rivers, streams, what? Remember, you can be *anything* you want.

Now, see yourself getting to your place of work and as you arrive think of the ideal people you choose to work with. What are their personalities like? What are they doing? *Imagine walking in to your own place of work and see yourself preparing for the day.* Think of your day and what you are doing for ideal job satisfaction.

Now imagine your evening, just as you want it to be. Where do you go? Who are you with? Is a quiet evening? Are you with friends? Are you relaxing? See your life as you really would like it.

The next day you wake up and discover it's the first day of your ideal holiday. Imagine your excitement. Where are you going? Think of the most idyllic way to spend your time, without limitations.

Your vision might be possible

Now come back to this moment and record the key visions that come to you. What qualities did you have? How did you feel about yourself? What did your home look like? What was your ideal occupation? Where did you go for your holiday?

Key visions

1.
2.
3.
4.
5.
6.
7.
8.
9.
10.

Now pick two aspects of your vision which you could aim for over a three or five year period. Pick one in your professional life and one in your personal life. Record them in the box below.

Then think of three probable roadblocks that stand in your way and of the actions you can take to overcome them. See what you get. It might be easier than you think:

Professional aspiration: ....

Roadblocks	Actions to overcome roadblocks
....	....
....	....
....	....

Personal aspiration: ....

Roadblocks	Actions to overcome roadblocks
....	....
....	....
....	....

Keep these points in mind all day, and you'll have an excellent chance of achieving them.

You can do it
In an audiotape interview with Janet Lim, whom I featured in *Secrets of the World's Top Sales Performers,* I asked what advice she would give to any manager or any parent who wanted to inspire others to reach their highest potential.

She thought for a moment then answered, 'You should tell them, "You can do it, You can do it, You can do it." She said we might have to repeat it six or seven times.

It doesn't matter whether they are facing a new job, a new habit they want to acquire or even a maths homework assignment. She is convinced that the first step to success is the belief that we can succeed.

Yet in order to break out of the comfort zone, we usually have to give the 'you can do it' message to ourselves.

Give yourself the message
Take one young man, Tony, who told me that he wanted to be a film producer. He had achieved marvellous success in film class, yet when he told his parents of this success, they remarked derogatorily, 'That's nice, Tony. What were your marks?' To make matters worse, when he told his cousin, the response was 'Who, *you*? A film producer?'.

His parents wanted him to be a plumber. While meaning well, they weren't supporting his vision and talent in life.

> If we want to change our patterns to lead to greater success, we have to give the 'you can do it' message to ourselves.

Stop the resistance

When we are holding ourselves back, we have to analyse why we are doing it.

Fear vs. Love

Last week in my motivation seminar in London, I told the attendees to notice the difference between fear and love. One holds us back, the other propels us forward.

Example:

One woman said she had a fear of speaking out at large meetings. I asked her what she feared. Her answer was, 'They might think I'm foolish.'

I responded , 'On the other hand, a younger woman might see you as a role model, or perhaps there would be an important executive in the room who would respect you and think, 'I want to have her on our team. 'Isn't that a possibility? Wouldn't you also feel better about yourself?'

'Yes,' she said. I could see that her analysis had given her a new perspective and infinitely more courage.

Analysis for change
Fear Motivation Thinking: They may think I'm foolish.

Love Motivation Thinking: I might inspire a younger person, or a colleague might respect me for my courage and conviction. Plus I know I'll feel good about myself when I do it.

The more we practise expanding the comfort zone in one area of life, the easier it is to expand it into other areas.

Take a moment now to question again. What would you do in life if you knew you couldn't fail at anything?

Action steps
What would you really like to do?
A.
B.
C.

What's holding you back?
A.
B.
C.

Action required to break out?
A.
B.
C.

The management application

Here's the situation that exists in management. Research has proven that our time spent in meetings breaks down like this: 80% discussing problems and causes of problems, but only 20% on possible solutions. When the researchers looked at it closer, they discovered even more disconcerting news. It looks like this:

Time spent in meetings

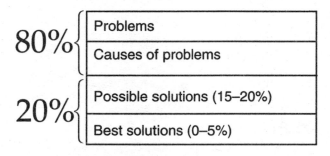

When managers become aware of this, they are usually quite appalled and realise the need for change. Armed with this information, they go back to their colleagues, make them aware of the statistics, and put a new emphasis on meeting agendas.

They try to reverse the time spent to look like this:

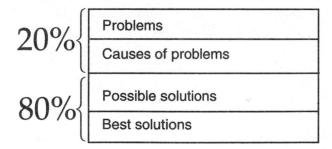

They realise that while we cannot ignore the problem, the problem *should not consume us*. We must learn what we can from the problem and then focus the majority of our time, energy and mental resources on the solution. Soon it becomes a habit to focus on solutions rather than problems alone.

Think of areas of your business in which the focus on problems blinds the path to solutions.

> The corporation is nothing more than a composite of individuals. They each bring their own strength with them, but also their 'limitation' thinking. It's our job as managers to reverse this.

Think now of problem areas that exist. Perhaps they've existed for some time. What action can you take to create a move towards 'solutions' thinking? Consider the following:

Steps to Solution Leadership
- Make people aware of the above statistics
- Commit to spending more meeting time on solutions
- Examine logical road blocks
- Examine psychological road blocks
- Visualise what solution there would be if there were no limitations, then see which solutions *can* be implemented.
- Don't let discussion drift away from solutions.
- Take a few moments now to list three actions you'll take at future meetings.

1. ....
2. ....
3. ....

This reversal towards possibilities and solutions can be applied to decision making in both business and personal life.

To be highly motivated we have to believe that there is virtually no road block that can't be overcome with flexibility, creativity and determination.

Motivation Action Sheet

Use the action section below to enhance your own
techniques and achievements.

Ideas for development:

1 Decide which areas of limitation thinking are blocking
   you from reaching your goals.

2 Where would you work, what would you do and where
   would your life take you if you could be anything you
   wanted to be?

3 Think about how long it has been since you 'took the
   plunge' for something you really want.

4 Analyse the limitation thinking at meetings. Decide what
   you can and will do to change it.

5 Other points as they relate to you (complete according to
   your needs).

Answers
- Of the above ideas, which one is likely to yield the
  best results for you?
- What percentage performance increase could
  realistically be expected?
- How long would it take:
  - to develop the idea?
  - to get results?
- Who would have to be involved?
- What date should you start?
- What is the first step you should take?

The confidence building process

The confidence building process can be used as a
motivational tool in the following areas:

- Self-esteem
- Employee confidence building
- Finding the positive side of life

The process can be used with
- Yourself
- Other people

To carry out this process you will need:
- A small notebook dedicated to this exercise, which
  fits in the pocket or handbag
- Two minutes per day, every day for two weeks,
  ideally at the end of the working day

The process

The process itself is deceptively simple yet it has profound
impact. Don't let its simplicity put you off. I've seen it help a
dynamic woman in her 70s to recherish life, a university
graduate to gain confidence at his first job, and I've used it
with myself and others to build morale.

You're likely to start seeing results as early as the third day,
and the effect of two complete weeks has a positive visible
impact for several years.

Try it now on yourself and see what you get. Then you'll be in a position to 'sell' the idea to other people.

You sit down at the end of a working day and reflect on the day's events.

Find two events that you enjoyed or got a sense of satisfaction from and record these.

The self-esteem application

After you record your two points for the day, ask yourself this question.

'What quality do I have which enabled me to enjoy that or to get a sense of satisfaction from it?'

Jot the quality down at the bottom of the page. Choose any word which seems right to you. It could be persistence, caring about people, creativity, love of challenge, sensitivity, communication skill, curiosity and so on. Now close the book. You're finished for today.

Tomorrow at the same time of day, you review the day's events and choose another two which you enjoyed or got satisfaction from.

You record these and decide what quality you had which enabled you to enjoy it. The quality can be the same or different from the day before.

Look for trends
By the third day you'll have six events and qualities and you'll start to see a trend building.

Self-esteem progress

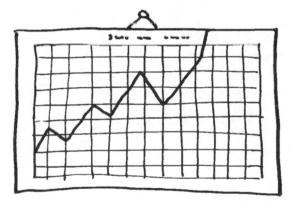

Look for the common factors in what you enjoyed and got satisfaction from. Did you like talking with people, and if so what was it that you enjoyed? Was it negotiating? Was it helping them find solutions? Was it the camaraderie of being on a team?

By the end of the two weeks you'll have a very clear understanding of your strengths and what you enjoy. You will have a new and very positive insight about yourself. This knowledge will have a profound impact on your self-esteem.

Here is an example:

Karen was in her 30s and wanted to interview for a meaningful job leading to a career in management, after some years out of the workforce raising children. Her self-esteem was far lower than she would have liked it to be.

She was afraid to pick up the telephone to prospective employers and job placement agencies. She used the small book process because she felt she needed to raise her self-esteem in order to convince herself first of her marketable value before she could convince someone else.

Here are her recordings. What trend do you see?

Day 1
Enjoyment/satisfaction events
1. Read psychology book and got new idea to implement
2. Enjoyed phone call with cabinet maker regarding modifications

Qualities relating to above
1. Good at focusing on implementation
2. Good at creating solutions

Day 2

Enjoyment/satisfaction events

1. Enjoyed talking with new person at adult education class
2. Satisfactions from re-organising driving schedule of three parents with co-operation from all

Qualities relating to above

1. Realisation that I activated the meeting and conversation
2. Working with people to create solutions

Day 3

Enjoyment/satisfaction events

1. Great satisfaction from speaking up at committee meeting to bring subject back on track
2. Enjoyed organising German-speaking get-together

Qualities relating to above

1. Ability to see main purpose. Ability to lead others
2. Ability to organise people and activate events

After only three days she had undeniable evidence that she was good at implementing ideas, organising events, clarifying purpose and leading people. These are perfect management skills.

After 14 days the evidence was even more undeniable, and she actually had more than sufficient self-esteem to approach prospective employers and agencies. She reported having more self-esteem than she could ever remember having.

The employee confidence building application

Let's look at ways to use the process with employees. Your situation could be similar to the one below, which I faced when I hired a university graduate. This was his first professional job. After one week I noticed that John's confidence was not as high as it needed to be to talk to senior executives on the telephone. I didn't have time for him to 'grow into the job'.

I needed him to take a giant leap. I wanted him to transfer his skills from university life to the job at once. Here's how I did it using two minutes a day with the confidence building process.

Let them pin-point their own strengths.
First I explained the process, saying that the purpose was for him to discover his own strengths. Then I explained exactly how to review the day and choose two things he enjoyed or got self-satisfaction from. I stressed that the two points

should definitely be what he himself valued, not what he thought I would value.

A few minutes later I reviewed the list with him. That was important because I was looking for events and qualities which could prove to John that he was good at speaking with high level executives on the telephone, which is what was needed from him.

Here's how it progressed. John came to me with the following:

> *Day 1*
> **Enjoyment/satisfaction events**
> 1. Enjoyed finding suitable prospective customers from Chamber of Commerce trade mission lists
> 2. Felt good about sitting in on meeting with Mr Barrett

On the first day I assisted with identifying the qualities: 'This is interesting – identifying the prospective customers. What did you like about it?'

John answered, 'I liked trying to figure out which ones were most likely to need our service. I looked at their industry and the details about their company.'

'What does that tell you about yourself?', I asked

'Hum, I suppose I like fact finding.'

'Yes, I agree. And that's an important quality in dealing with high level executives. They will value that in you when you work with them,' John wrote down 'Good at fact finding' as the first quality.

Let them record it ...

By letting the employee write it down, you will be helping him or her reinforce *their* qualities and thus *their* confidence. It is he or she, not you, who needs the quick confidence building.

'Now let's look at point two,' I said. 'What was it that you liked about sitting in on the meeting with Mr Barrett?'

'I suppose I liked trying to figure out why he was here and what he hoped to gain,' answered John.

'Ah,' I interjected. 'That's very important. I'm glad you've seen that about yourself. Imagine how happy these executives will feel about talking with you because you're trying to figure out what they need. This is a great help to them. What more could they ask?'

Sometime later John told me that he left the office that night on such a high that he couldn't sleep.

His enthusiasm the next day was boundless. He reasoned that I was his boss, so if I believed in him, he should believe in himself. After all, I should know.

After three or four days of this there was no holding him back. I practically needed two telephones to keep him going.

Choosing the correct strength

Naturally you'll choose a confidence building area which is needed by your department. But you need not feel too selfish about this because the confidence area you chose to work on will spread to other areas of your employee's job and life. You'll get higher performance; the employee will increase his or her self-development and satisfaction with life.

When you use this process:
- You gain
- The employee gains
- The corporation gains

Finding the positive side of life

A very dynamic client of mine attended my seminar on confidence building and decided to apply it to seeing life in a more positive way.

I knew her to be a very positive person, and I wondered frankly whether the process could help as I didn't see much room for improvement.

After a few days she called me to say that she was astounded with her findings. On the first day she sat for 20 minutes reviewing the day. She could find nothing positive, nothing she enjoyed, nothing satisfying. The day, as she saw it, had been full of problems to be solved, annoyances to be overcome. For 20 minutes she probed and probed and found nothing – absolutely nothing. She was ready to give up.

Suddenly another thing popped into her mind – a letter she had received from a treasured friend abroad, reminiscing about their recent time together. She remembered that as she had read the letter, she was filled with gratitude about the excitement of life and friendship. Next she remembered another positive event and another.

She wondered how the negative points of her day could have blocked the memory of the day's positive points in her mind for 20 minutes? It seemed impossible.

This realisation heightened her determination to keep at the process.

The next night she reported that the negative factors again took predominance, but not for as long a period.

Again, she was astounded at how the mind could be so stubbornly stuck to the negative, when in fact there was so much that was good. Yet the mind, by pushing these back, leaves us in a negative mental spiral.

Firm up the muscles of the mind
She persisted the third day and found that she could now more easily bring the positive events up in her mind. She decided that the process of positive recall in the brain is analogous to muscles in the body that needed firming up. Without use, they become weak and ineffective.

The conclusion is this. If this person who was already very positive found benefit from this process, imagine the benefits that await the rest of us.

Where to apply it
Take today to decide who to use this motivation process with. Will it be yourself? Will it be others? Think also of the outcome desired; self-esteem, confidence building, finding the positive side of life.

Application	
Who (self/others)	Outcome desired
....	....
....	....
....	....
....	....
....	....

Remember, you have the power within you to influence your world around you.

Motivation Action Sheet

Use the action section below to enhance your own techniques and achievements.

Ideas for development:

1 Build your own self-esteem with this method.

2 Raise employees' confidence.

3 Heighten your morale.

4 Look for trends in your strengths.

5 Encourage employees to pinpoint their own strengths with this method.

6 Other points as they relate to you (complete according to your needs).

Answers
- Of the above ideas, which one is likely to yield the best results for you?
- What percentage performance increase could realistically be expected?
- How long would it take:
  - to develop the idea?
  - to get results?
- Who would have to be involved?
- What date should you start?
- What is the first step you should take?

The three part reinforcement process

How many teachers did you ever have who really, really motivated you? Probably one or two. How many managers ever really, really motivated you? Again, probably only one or two. And when you think of it, weren't they the ones who encouraged you or showed you something positive in yourself?

There are few people who make others see the best in themselves. Those few who do, have people who will follow them anywhere because this is such a rare and treasured commodity.

What is this rare commodity? It is the skill of positive reinforcement.

In doing work with thousands of seminar attendees around the world we've developed a three-part process which is effective with every culture, every age group, and every industry group. You can master it in a day in four steps.

1. Choose several people you want to motivate from business or personal life
2. Write out a statement of positive reinforcement for each from the pages which follow
3. Test the process on an ad lib basis with those around you who are not on the list in order to build your expertise – the children, the caretaker, the dog, the postman
4. Telephone two from your list and give the reinforcement. The reaction you'll get will be so reinforcing for you that you'll continue without hesitation

The process

The three-part positive reinforcement process:

1. Tell the other person exactly what action they did correctly
2. Tell them how the action helped you or the organisation
3. Express your honest and sincere appreciation

Points two and three can be reversed in order, depending on how it suits you and the situation. You can thank them and then tell how it helped or vice versa.

On the pages that follow, we give you examples from six different situations. Use these for inspiration for your own people. Undoubtedly you'll think of people and situations as you read these. Jot down the names and ideas so that you can implement them immediately.

Chances are that the rewards to yourself of practising positive reinforcement will be greater than you can imagine. Once you start it, you will want to use it in every situation.

The employee application

To improve performance
The situation is this. We have an employee who is important in the chain of events, but one of his skill areas falls short of the required performance. It is his lack of attention to detail.

Each time he communicates a message, there is an error in it caused by this lack of attention to detail. We find that packages are going to wrong addresses at the wrong time, messages are getting confused and so on.

He is valuable in other skill areas such as making good contact with people and we want to help him improve in this area of detail in order to meet the job requirements. Our objective is to motivate him, not *demotivate* him.

We look for even the *slightest* improvement or any sign that he's handled detail better. Then we use the three part process.

The Process: Raising Performance

- *Repeat the correct action exactly*
  'John, yesterday when you wrote that list of
  addresses down, you carefully double-checked
  them with me,' we say.

- *Express your honest, sincere appreciation*
  'I appreciate that extra trouble you took.'

- *Tell them how that action helped you or the
  organisation*
  'It will help us to be accurate the first time, and
  considering how busy we are here, that's vital.
  Thanks, John.'

The positive reinforcement will only take us 30 seconds to
say, but it will linger for hours with the employee.

By acknowledging the *correct* behaviour, we are calling attention to it. After we do this two, three or four times, the acknowledgement will be ingrained. The employee will be soon checking the details as a matter of course.

Avoid this mistake
Some people misinterpret this process as being one in which they tell the employee what *should* have been done. They substitute the correct action taken with the correct action they would like to see.

This is *not* positive reinforcement. It's another type of communication exercise which draws attention to what was not accomplished. It is reinforcement of negative behaviour which is demotivating for the employee.

The danger is that:

- They can feel you are ungrateful for all that they *have* done, or
- They can feel they are hopelessly unable to achieve

Both are demotivating.

'John, I noticed yesterday that you didn't double-check the addresses with me. You must do this in the future because it's important to be accurate.'

This is not positive reinforcement.

The best way to change behaviour *and* motivate is to show the employee proof that they have already succeeded and that you endorse what they *can* do. You prove it by picking an incident in which they *have* done it. That endorsement leads to more of the same.

The loyalty application

The situation is this. We have a high-flying sales executive who outperforms the others on the team by 50% and more. She is highly motivated and we know she could move to other jobs for more money or career opportunities. We would like to maintain her performance and keep her with the company.

First, before we give positive reinforcement, we think about her situation and ask ourselves what kind of acknowledgement she wants.

Chances are that she's working hard, has perfected her sales skills and keeps her motivation up. Now what is it that really puts her head and shoulders above the rest? We want to give her acknowledgement for this special skill or attribute. We decide that her decisive quality is determination

Secondly, we know it's important to reinforce only one thing at a time. Since we want to maintain her performance and keep her loyalty to the company, we decide to reinforce the determination behind her performance. We know she'll have that loyalty to us for seeing the best in her will be a definite outcome.

We proceed as follows:

The Process: Raising Loyalty

- *Repeat the correct action exactly*

  'Julie, I want to commend you on your consistent high sale results. I know it's not a magical process. It's no accident that you're 50% above everyone else. It takes unrelenting determination to achieve what you've achieved. Determination to make the appointments every day, determination to close every sale, determination to keep perfecting skills,' we say.

- *Tell how the action helped you or the organisation*

  'That's a wonderful role model for the others on the team. They may never be able to reach your level but step by step, by seeing your determination, they'll be able to improve their determination and improve their results and job satisfaction.'

- *Express honest, sincere appreciation*

  'Thanks for your contribution, Julie. We're lucky to have you on our team.'

It's said that if we show people the best in themselves, they will follow us anywhere.

The world around us is filled with people who are used to expressing negativity and doubt. Others are contained in their own shell, their energy going towards self-survival. You might be the only person who develops the skill to motivate the people around you.

The negative type

The situation is this. We go to a committee meeting for a fund-raising project, and there is much diversity of opinion about the venue, the ticket price, and even the date of the event. The chairman is ready to throw his hands up in despair and resign the post if people don't consolidate.

One person in particular, Arthur, is a rabble-rouser. While he stated several good ideas, he also stirred up things by wanting to look at the negative side of every suggestion made. Therefore, the meeting is having more negative than positive conclusions.

We assess the situation and decide that positive reinforcement is necessary to change the output of the rabble rouser, otherwise we *and* the chairman *and* half of the committee will abandon the project. But the project is needed by the committee and we want it to succeed.

Therefore, at the coffee break, we go to Arthur the rabble-rouser, and start a friendly conversation.

In the meantime our mind is racing through the dialogue of the evening looking for good points to reinforce which meet the group's objective of a positive conclusion.

At last we remember one specific action and we use that:

The Process: Reducing Negativity

* *Repeat the correct action exactly*
  'Arthur, I was thinking of the time tonight that you supported the chairman, after the majority vote on the venue,' we say.

* *Tell how that action helped you or the organisation*
  'I noticed that your support had a positive effect on the group. Everyone felt good to have one thing settled.'

* *Express honest, sincere appreciation*
  'Thanks, It's good to work on committees with supportive people because we achieve a lot.'

You may feel that this approach is a bit transparent and that Arthur or types like him will see right through it.

But remember that for many people, their behaviour is more subsconscious than conscious. So far, the attention they've had in life has been for their unusual behaviour, in this case rabble-rousing. *We are drawing attention to another behaviour which they can perceive as noble and worthy of consciously repeating.*

The volunteer application

There are thousands of very worthy organisations around us in which people volunteer their time: chambers of commerce, church groups, community groups, charities, committees, service clubs.

Think what added impact they could make if their members could be more motivated. Perhaps you are the person to do that. You don't have to be in a position of leadership to motivate people. It can be your unique contribution to the organisation. The loyalty and good you will build will be profoundly rewarding. And you *become* the leader.

To enhance performance
The situation is this. You have many members who come into your group and show enthusiasm for the first few months, then fade away. It seems that all the work is left to the same people, year in and year out.

Your goal is to get more people co-operating and giving their time. You just decide that it's time for a change and you take on the challenge yourself.

Start at base line '0'
From this point forward, you decide that you'll give every member positive reinforcement for *some* action they've taken. It doesn't matter how small this action was. You start

with a base line of '0', that is 'zero contribution'. Anything above that you should consider to be a contribution.

What did each member do? Did they attend? Good. That's noteworthy, isn't it? No one *has* to come. They could, in fact, drop out. That's their option if they're not motivated. We're the ones asking for change, not them. We have to do the motivating and loyalty building. It's important not to be judgemental.

The process: Increasing Participation
- ***Repeat the correct action exactly***
  'Ted, thanks for coming tonight,' we say.

- ***Express honest, sincere appreciation***
  'I know it's tough after a long day at work.'

- ***Tell how that action helped you or the organisation***
  'It really helps us to succeed when we have busy members like you who make the extra effort to come. Thanks.'

In volunteer groups as well as in business, negativity can creep in and people feel their work isn't appreciated. It takes positive reinforcement to counter this. Think now of what else you can reinforce with any individual members. What about committee work?

The Process: Continuing Contribution

- ***Repeat the correct action exactly***
  'Alice, we'd like to thank you for your efforts on the telephone committee.'

- ***Tell how it helped you or the organisation***
  'At the board meeting last week we discussed the fact that attendance at meetings is up 30% over last year. We're sure it's due to your work on the telephone committee.'

- ***Express honest, sincere appreciation***
  'Thanks, Alice. I know it's not easy to make the time and we're all very grateful to you.'

It's important to recognise every member's input. I can guarantee that if you reinforce this, within two months you'll have a completely different atmosphere and enthusiasm level. I've seen it time and time again.

Think now of the groups you belong to. What could you do to be a catalyst for positive change?

The boss application

The situation is this. Your boss is always hassled and you want more time to talk uninterrupted.

To gain support

Your purpose is to gain support, so you use the three part process to reinforce something you like and want more of in the way of support.

Therefore you:

The Process: Gaining Support

- ### *Repeat the correct action exactly*
  'Harry, do you remember three months ago when you took time to go to lunch to discuss the Egyptian project?' you say.

- ### *Tell how it helped you or the organisation*
  'I want you to know how much I valued that chance to talk without interruption. It helped me afterwards to work with more clarity and it speeded up the whole process.'

- ### *Express honest, sincere appreciation*
  'I know your time is torn in all directions so I wanted to take the opportunity to let you know I appreciated it. Thanks.'

Remember that bosses don't get as much positive recognition as they would like either.

Naturally, this process can be used for anyone you want support from, not only your boss. Just think of a time when they did something that you appreciated in the way of support and reinforce it.

The partner application

The situation is this. You're sitting together at a cafe in Paris or London or Prague or Los Angeles. It crosses your mind that these occasions are too few and far between. You have two choices. You can lambast yourself and your partner for not taking more time alone together or you can use positive reinforcement. Which one is likely to get the best results? (Hint: the old way doesn't usually work very well for most people, does it?)

The Process: Relationships
- ***Repeat the correct action exactly***
  Michael/Michelle: 'Isn't it fantastic sitting here like this together? I'm so glad we took the time to do it,' we say.
- ***Express your honest, sincere appreciation***
  'Thanks for rearranging your schedule so that we could come. I know it took an effort.'

- **How it helped you or the organisation**
  'It's really great to stop and celebrate now and again.
  It makes me realise that's what we work for.'

Tips for perfecting the process

1. Repeat the correct action precisely so that it's clear what action you refer to.
2. Include only the part of the action which you wish to reinforce.
3. Reinforce only one action at a time.
4. Repeat the reinforcement process often. Choose different actions relating to the same performance you wish to reinforce, until you are happy with the level.
5. When the desired level is reached, reinforce occasionally.

Think now of what you want to reinforce, and with whom:

Action Steps

Who

....

Repeat the correct action exactly

....

Tell how it helped you or the organisation

....

Express honest, sincere appreciation

....

Motivation Action Sheet

Use the action section below to enhance your own techniques and achievements.

Ideas for development:

1 Use this method to improve employee performance.

2 Use to build loyalty from others.

3 Use this to turn around negativity.

4 Use with volunteer and community groups to encourage participation.

5 Use this with your partner to encourage the behaviour you desire.

6 Other points as they relate to you (complete according to your needs).

Answers

- Of the above ideas, which one is likely to yield the best results for you?
- What percentage performance increase could realistically be expected?
- How long would it take:
  – to develop the idea?
  – to get results?
- Who would have to be involved?
- What date should you start?
- What is the first step you should take?

The dolphin process

Do you want to motivate your employees, your family, or even your local sports team to raise their performance level? If so, you can use a process used by dolphin trainers which has proved to be very effective in motivating people to improve their performance.

The process

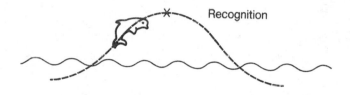

Recognition

In training the dolphin, the trainer analyses the current skill or performance level of each dolphin. They then pick the highest level which the dolphin can jump and wait until the dolphin reaches that level in its jump. When that high point is reached, a whistle is blown. The whistle acts as a reinforcement for the dolphin to achieve that level more often.

When the dolphin stabilises at that level, the trainer raises the level at which the whistle is blown. When the dolphin reaches that new high level in any jump, the whistle recognition acts as a reinforcement to achieve that higher level more often. The trainer repeats the process, stabilising each level, moving the performance gradually up.

The teacher application

For better progress and enjoyment
Let's look at a variety of ways this can be used to motivate people to raise their performance. One language teacher uses this instant reinforcement to improve the pronunciation of his students in learning foreign languages.

He has a pleasant sounding buzzer he rings each time the student pronounces the 'e' sound properly. When the 'e' is stabilised, he moves onto the 'a' sound, and so on. Their progress is fast and they become more encouraged more quickly.

The drop-out level of his students is considerably lower than it was before he started the system, his graduates have a reputation for excellence which reflects favourably on his school, and, most importantly, his students really enjoy learning. They report much more confidence and motivation.

For faster skill building
When I train instructors to run our courses, I use the system in this way. Each instructor has a turn to make his or her presentation and I observe their skills.

First I give them positive feedback on everything they do well in their presentation – voice level, eye contact, friendliness and so on.

Then I choose one area for improvement and they concentrate on that in their next round of presentations. Each time they succeed in the improvement, they get a thumbs up signalling success from one of us at the back of the room. When the thumbs up comes from their fellow trainers as well, the impact is raised.

When they reach the level of performance necessary in that area, then we change the focus to another area, such as voice modulation or whatever needs improving. Within an extraordinarily short period their skill level moves up.

The process is almost unbelievable. The head of one of our training centres told the new instructors, 'You changed in front of my very eyes. I can hardly believe it's possible.'

The employee application

One manager used this process to help her employee, Martin, communicate his ideas more often at meetings. The employee was reluctant to speak out for fear of being wrong or being ridiculed, yet his ideas were often superior to those of his colleagues.

Without telling him what the desired performance was, the manager drafted an improvement schedule for what she hoped she could motivate him to achieve.

The important schedule looked like this, stage by stage

1. Speak out, even one to five words: stabilise;
2. Express a complete idea or suggestion: stabilise;
3. Express an opinion: stabilise;
4. Defend his position: stabilise;
5. Make a presentation: stabilise;
6. Make a presentation and take questions afterwards, defending his position: stabilise.

At the next meeting she watched carefully for *any* comment he might make. Her goal, remember, was to reinforce even one to five words he might say. She knew from past experience that this was likely to be his maximum performance level. Finally it came. After one colleague expressed his view, Martin added, 'Yes, I've observed that too'.

Give instant reinforcement
She was quick to give instant reinforcement. She said to the group, 'Martin has observed that too. That's important. Now let's delve into this issue further. If anyone has any observations on this area during the week, I would like a report back on it. Thank you, Martin.'

Thus his speaking out was reinforced. After several meetings he was speaking out more readily and therefore she decided it was time to move her reinforcement up to stage two, that of expressing his opinion. She waited for that and when it came she reinforced it in a similar way.

She continued stage by stage to stabilise the performance, then move the reinforcement up to a higher plateau.

Her planning and reinforcement looked like this:

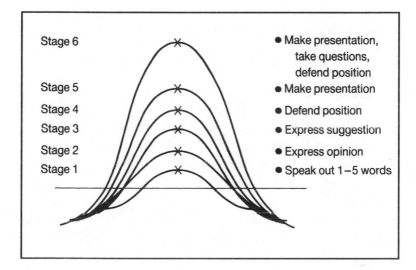

Stage 6 — ● Make presentation, take questions, defend position
Stage 5 — ● Make presentation
Stage 4 — ● Defend position
Stage 3 — ● Express suggestion
Stage 2 — ● Express opinion
Stage 1 — ● Speak out 1–5 words

Stabilise each stage

From the above example we see the importance of two aspects:

- Plan your reinforcement levels ahead of time
- Stick with the reinforcement of *each* stage until you are confident it is stabilised

The manager reported the importance of reinforcing the first stage securely. This required the most patience on her part. After that the progress was quicker.

In this employee's case:

- the first stage required six reinforcements
- the second stage required four
- the third required three
- the fourth required three
- the fifth required two
- the sixth required two

After that she gave sporadic reinforcement to the employee which maintained the level.

Thus we see that with a total of only 20 reinforcements, the employee went from inadequate to excellent in his verbal contributions. That's an incredible feat hardly achievable with any other known method.

The importance of stages
Think about the process and see what you observe to be the key elements. Where would it be likely to fall apart? What pressure points should we watch for?

Certainly the planning of the stages is important. Notice, for example, that the manager chose to reinforce Martin's expression of a suggestion and his expression of an opinion as two different segments. This builds confidence.

Had she tried to achieve the same results with only four stages of reinforcement with that employee, without such finely divided increments, he may not have succeeded.

However, with another employee with more skill or confidence, she may have been able to use only four increment stages, either leaving out some or starting her reinforcement at stage three.

Set the level right

Thus it's important to put emphasis on our planning of increments, making each level achievable for each particular employee according to their skill and confidence level.

Applications

Think about the people you might want to motivate to a higher performance level. Are there members of your firm, family, community or clubs? Whose skill or performance level do you want to enhance?

Take today to write the ideal skill or performance level you would like them to achieve, then list the increments you could reinforce:

Application Plan

Person 1

Name   *Ideal skill level to achieve*

....

Increments to reinforce

....

....

....

....

....

Person 2

Name   *Ideal skill level to achieve*

....

Increments to reinforce

....

....

....

....

....

How long to reinforce

Many people worry that the reinforcement will have to go
on forever. They also worry that the skill area or behaviour
will slip backwards without reinforcement.

This, fortunately, is *not* the case. Once we learn to ride a
bicycle, we don't need to ride it every day. Now and again is
enough. So it is with reinforcement.

Self-application

The following is an example of how someone applied the
process to improve their own situation. As you read it, you
might be tempted to think it's a trivial issue, not worth
bothering about. But remember that life is really a composite
of individual issues. If we can improve one issue
dramatically as Jenny did, it impacts positively on ourselves
and the people around us.

As you read, look at the care Jenny took to analyse her
situation and plan each increment accordingly.

Jenny's problem was that she work up in a negative frame of
mind every morning. It took her a good 45 minutes before
she was ready to face the world.

She hated this way of starting the day and decided to use
this process to see if she could change her situation. Her
target was to have 30 seconds or less of negativity each
morning instead of 45 minutes.

She analysed the thoughts and actions of her negative frame
of mind in order to figure out how to reverse each one.

These were her irrational throughts which seemed rational
when her alarm went off:

Example
- Oh, no
- I can't handle the day. Too much to do, not enough
  time.
- Why am I in this situation? I want to escape
- It's too much effort to get dressed
- I never have time for anything I really want to do.

She then set up the following stage increments:

Block out negativity: Stage 1
She decided that she needed to start with blocking out all
negative thoughts until she had her first sip of coffee. She
bought a timer for her coffee machine so that it would be
ready instantly.

Block out negativity: Stage 2
Then she moved up to her next increment. 'Don't worry
about getting dressed until after your shower.'

Block out negativity: Stage 3
Then she decided on her third increment – 'Get oxygen
flowing to brain'. She would go straight from the shower to
an *easy to open* window, open it and take a few deep breaths.

Block out negativity: Stage 4
Still she wasn't sure these three steps were enough. She also
knew that once she was involved in a task that engaged her
mind, she was fine.

She remembered that she liked to write short thank-you notes to friends, but felt she never had time. She decided to make that her fourth stage. This would engage her mind without taxing it with decisions.

She reckoned that the time she usually spent feeling depressed could be diverted to this task and she could still leave the house in time for work.

Next she planned how many days it would take to stabilise each stage. Her projection looked like this:

1st stage (6 days): Coffee – think of nothing else
2nd stage (6 days): Coffee and shower – think of nothing else
3rd stage (10 days): Coffee, shower and fresh air – think of nothing else
4th stage (4 days): Coffee, shower, fresh air, write thank-you note

It seemed like a lot of work, but she didn't like the alternative of waking up each morning in such a negative stage. She was motivated by the realisation that if she stuck with the old system, over the same period of 26 days, she would have accumulated $19^1/_2$ hours of demotivating misery. Thus, it was worth a try.

In actual fact, her results were better than her prediction. By the second day she was doing the coffee, the shower and the thank-you note. She said that it seemed that, by having a positive, step-by-step progression of things to do, the mind was keen to move from one to the next.

Try this exercise

Take a minute now to think of how you could apply the process to your own situation. What performance or achievement level would you like to reach?

Action Plan
Ideal level to achieve:

....

Increments   *Predicted*
                                       repetitions
                                       needed

....

....

....

....

....

In this self-application process, you'll have to be the coach and the subject. This means you'll have to set everything up ahead of time.

In Jenny's case she had to prepare for stage 1 by buying a timer for the coffee maker, and then filling it in the night before. She had to put the thank-you notes in a readily accessible place. Make a list and get everything ready for every stage before you start stage 1.

Take today to think about this process and decide how else to use it. Will it be with colleagues, with yourself, or both? Decide when and what to do.

Motivation Action Sheet

Use the action section below to enhance your own techniques and achievements.

Ideas for development:

1 Use this method for faster skill building, better progress and enjoyment.

2 Remember to give instant reinforcement.

3 Stabilise each stage.

4 Set the right level for reinforcement.

5 Use it to change your own morale and behaviour too.

6 Other points as they relate to you (complete according to your needs).

Answers
- Of the above ideas, which one is likely to yield the best results for you?
- What percentage performance increase could realistically be expected?
- How long would it take:
  - to develop the idea?
  - to get results?
- Who would have to be involved?
- What date should you start?
- What is the first step you should take?

The anti-procrastination process

Let's look at a typical procrastination syndrome. Ron had a report to write which was hanging over his head. He didn't know why but he couldn't seem to get started. He blamed it on lack of motivation.

The root of all procrastination is the mind's belief that the job is too big or too demanding to start it now.

When the mind says that something is *too demanding*, what it really means is that it is *not routine*.

> **The mind prefers us to do tasks we are used to because it can put us onto automatic pilot to accomplish them. Then it can get on with what it loves most, that is, daydreaming, fantasising and reliving conversations or events of the past.**

Make it look routine

When we try to engage in a new, non-routine task, the mind has to turn off the automatic pilot and give full attention to this new task. Since this distracts it from its favourite pastime, it sends us messages which encourage us to procrastinate: 'too much bother, too much bother', or 'that takes too long, you don't have time now', or 'do it tomorrow when you feel up to it'.

We have to entice the mind into participating and the best way of doing this is to show it that the new task won't be so bad.

The closer we can make it seem to its old patterns of operation, the more readily it will accept it.

The most effective way to do this is to break the job up into small distinct segments. The mind won't object to tackling a small familiar piece. It can do that in automatic.

The smaller we make the pieces so that it can operate in automatic, the better it likes it. Therefore, we create more chance of starting and finishing.

Get the facts
What if a segment has unknowns, you might ask? This is an important question because the mind will want to avoid unknowns at all costs.

What if we don't know how to tackle a segment? What if the facts are missing?

Let's look at a typical example. We have a task, we've divided it into pieces, and we discover one unknown which our mind is likely to rebel against. That unknown is 'lack of financial information.'

We look for possible sources of information, put it into a list and plan to tackle it one by one. Our list looks like this:

- Ask experts
- Read about it
- Ask friends

But the mind's not very happy about that either because it's not clear who to call or where to go to read.

Sweep away all unknowns

So we segment it again by thinking of possible 'who and where' options. This time it likes most of the results because there are few unknowns. It can be tackled in automatic.

Ron's list looks like this for his report writing:

Experts
- Call Joe, my accountant
- Call the man I met last week at the Chamber of Commerce

Read
- Go to library on Cromwell Road
- Buy magazine at railway station

Friends
- Call Jane – she runs a business
- Call Andy – he has a good accountant

The mind looks at this but it's still not very happy with one.

It doesn't like the idea of the Chamber of Commerce man at all because it doesn't know where to find his phone number.

'You don't expect me to find the number,' the mind protests. 'No, no of course not,' we answer. 'I'll get it for you.'

Push the starter button

And so we segment it even further.

Call Chamber of Commerce man:

- Look for card in briefcase
- Look for card in card file
- Ask Andy if he knows number
- Abandon if three above fail

This time the mind likes it because it can handle those three on automatic. There are no unknowns.

But if we were to stop here with our instructions to the mind, we would never get started. Why? Because the mind hasn't had its command on *when* to do it. Therefore we need to add dates and times and create a chart for it, as follows:

ANTI-PROCRASTINATION FORMULA

Goal:
...............Write Report...............

A. segments	B. Subsegments	C. Action dates
Call Joe	Get his number	Tomorrow – Monday
	– Try Briefcase	
	– Try Card File	Now – Sunday
	– Ask Andy	
Call Man Chamber		Mon 10 AM
Go Library		Mon Lunch
Buy Magazine		Mon RR Station
Call Jane		Tonight – Sun
Call Andy		Tonight – Sun

0340737611.I.L.T.UK.PS

Any goal needs segmenting. The major road block which leads to procrastination is lack of segmenting.

That was the situation Ron faced over his report writing. Once he segmented it, he saw clearly why he wasn't motivated to start. It's because there were missing pieces. Subconsciously these missing pieces caused him worry but

without identifying it, he couldn't turn the worry into
constructive action.

Remember who is master
We sometimes forget that we are master of our own minds.

To nudge the mind in a new direction, such as to undertake
a new task, requires conscious effort from us. In other
words, we have to tell it what to do or it will automatically
do something else. The best way to get it to take action is
through segmenting.

> For the best success, segment into the smallest, most
> distinct pieces possible

Try the process yourself using the blank chart which follows
to segment a task which you've been procrastinating over or
which is particularly important to you. Complete it as
follows:

A.   Fill in every component part you can think of on the A
     line first

B.   Only use the B column if there are loose ends on the A
     column – you don't have the phone number, the
     materials, the knowledge, etc.

C.   After A and B are finished, decide on schedule for C,
     keeping the time-frame as short as possible while not
     overwhelming. Then transfer the actions to a diary or
     'to do' list for each appropriate day

You may want to photocopy the sheet for use on various projects in the future, and keep these on hand.

ANTI-PROCRASTINATION FORMULA
Goal:
....

A. Segments	B. Subsegments	C. Action dates
....	....	....
	....	....
....	....	....
	....	....
....	....	....
	....	....
....	....	....
	....	....
....	....	....
	....	....
....	....	....
	....	....
....	....	....
	....	....
....	....	....

© Christine Harvey

Motivation Action Sheet

Use the action section below to enhance your own techniques and achievements.

Ideas for development:

1 Stop procrastination by making the job seem routine.

2 Get all the facts.

3 Sweep away all unknowns.

4 Learn to eliminate the mind's excuses.

5 Press the starter button.

6 Others points as they relate to you (complete according to your needs).

Answers

- Of the above ideas, which one is likely to yield the best results for you?
- What percentage performance increase could realistically be expected?
- How long would it take:
  - to develop the idea?
  - to get results?
- Who would have to be involved?
- What date should you start?
- What is the first step you should take?

The goal focus process

It's true that there are only 24 hours in a day. Why is it then that some people seem to accomplish so much, while others can't, no matter how hard they try? It's the same 24 hours for both.

When we focus time and energy in a specific direction, we achieve a lot.

But because life is like a smorgasbord of possibilities, the danger is that we can reach in this direction and that without focus, ending up with an interesting but not very productive hodge-podge of results.

Let's look at what blocks us.

Urgent versus important

Walter Blackburn, an instructor of the Dale Carnegie methods of motivation, stresses the importance of realising the difference between *important* and *urgent*.

We might be hounded by a supplier who tries to get us on the telephone four times in one day. On the fourth call, we start to feel it must be urgent and therefore we take the call. But in fact, in terms of our priorities its importance is low.

Everyone's day is full of these urgencies and distractions. Yet the people who achieve the most do so because they focus on the steps that lead to their goal.

Don't believe there is time for everything
One wise individual said, 'On the day we die, no matter how hard we worked, we will still be thinking of things we *could* have done.'

Since there is not enough time to do everything, we have to choose our path consciously, not be taken down it by default.

The choice is ours
Most people think the culprit in life is lack of time. In actual fact, the culprit is abdication of responsibility over making choices.

Watching television brings relaxation. That's a reward. For the same hour per day that we devote to watching TV, which adds up to seven hours per week, we could write a book and have it finished in six months or learned to play tennis well. These are different rewards. The choice is ours.

It's important to come to terms with this. Some people, for example, tell me that they think I'm hard-working. They look at the output and think it must have been hard work. But it's not. It's a matter of doing, in the same time, actions directly connected with priority goals rather than actions which divert and dilute the output. In other words:

> Twenty actions connected to 2 goals further those goals more than 20 actions connected to 20 goals

Here are three examples of what can happen.

Example 1

Ian has a reputation for being late to every meeting. His own perception of himself is that he's *just* on time. His behaviour is such that he catches planes with 30 seconds to spare; sometimes they hold the plane while he runs to the gate. His colleagues have stopped travelling with him and his wife is in despair. They can't stand the stress.

Yet Ian's *perception* of himself is that he's very productive. With the vision that life is an endless choice of possibilities, let's do an experiment and follow Ian around his office prior to his important airport meeting with a customer and their flight together that leaves at 2pm.

It's 11.00 and he feels pretty good. The drive to the airport takes one hour if traffic is light. He looks at his watch; time for one more phone call. After the phone call, he heads for the copier, sees a stack of files for tomorrow's meeting and stops to put them on a shelf.

On the way down the hall he passes Joe who is rarely in his office, and stops to discuss an upcoming proposal that has a deadline two weeks away.

He continues on his way to the copier, then heads quickly back to his office to collect his coat and briefcase. It's 12.30. His secretary tells him that Mr Barnes is holding from Australia, and he takes the call so as not to be rude.

It is now 12.38. With one hour minimum to get to the airport, it will be 1.38. Then he needs time to park and run to the terminal. The preflight meeting is long past. He'll barely have time to check in. 'Oh well' he consoles himself, 'my colleague will understand.' What pattern do you see?

Don't confuse opportunity with objective
Example 2
Larry is a neophyte salesman. He goes on a business trip with his boss who is an expert in selling. The boss says they must devote themselves to making phone calls to prospects from the hotel between appointments.

Larry is a great networker and he decides, without consulting his boss, to invite some local people he knows to the hotel to meet his boss and make a presentation about their product. This is a favour he's long promised them, and it's a wonderful opportunity while they are in town.

The friends duly arrive to do their presentation and afterwards Larry's boss is shocked. He views the situation as one in which Larry has lost his sense of purpose, which was to devote himself to gaining prospects. Secondly, the boss is surprised that Larry didn't recognise the need to devote himself to learning salesmanship techniques on this rare opportunity of being together.

Don't settle for small rewards
Example 3
Laura is a business owner, very successful but under a lot of stress. She's attending a weekend conference and her intention is to spend as much time as possible with other conference delegates in order to relax and meet new people.

She has one hour between sessions to socialise, but decides to nip upstairs to her room first to freshen up. She changes clothes, tidies her hair, tucks a few things back into her suitcase and sits down for a glass of water.

She makes a quick call home, then decides to change her shoes for the next session.

She then returns downstairs and finds there's only 10 minutes left before the session is to start. She manages to talk to one or two people, but she's left feeling disappointed that there's not enough time left to socialise as she'd hoped. Yet those were her choices. She settled for small rewards.

Don't fog your main objective
What is the common thread in these three patterns of operation? The pattern we see is that too many possibilities can obscure the main objective.

Ian did everything that needed to be done, but without priority. Larry was blinded by options and misguided by loyalties at inappropriate times. He was confusing opportunity with objective. Laura sacrificed her goal for small comforts with smaller rewards. They were all caught in the fog of options, without goal focus.

What other beliefs keep us in the fog? Many people fear that if they focus on goals, they will miss out on the rest of 'life', or that they will lose their creativity and spontaneity.

What they overlook is that they can use their creativity and spontaneity on those specific actions which lead them to their goal, just as well as they can use them on anything else.

Taking a rational look

It helps to look at a list and ask which apply:

> **Goal Setting: Typical Roadblocks**
> - Confusing important with urgent
> - Wanting to accomplish everything
> - Not defining our goal
> - Fear that we'll lose out on something better
> - Fear of loss of spontaneity and creativity

What conclusions do you reach? Why not rate yourself on a scale of 1 to 10 to see where you stand in each area? Give yourself a 10 if you never block yourself from your goal and a 1 if you often do. See what you get.

Blocks to focus	Rating
• I never confuse important and urgent	....
• I never think I should be able to accomplish everything	....
• I always define my goal	....
• I never fear losing out on something better	....
• I never worry that I'll lose spontaneity if I am goal focused	....
(Total out of 50)	_____

How did you score? Where can you improve?

Now we come to the point of choice. Shall we leave the situation as it is, or change it? What rewards could we expect from change? Would it be worth it? If so, look at the processes we've covered in all the chapters and decide which you'll use.

Area for improvement (Select from list of roadblocks above)	*Process* (Choose from those in previous chapters)
....	....
....	....
....	....
....	....

Do it now

The next step in the goal focus process is getting down to it.

I remember a client of mine who had a plaque on her office wall reading:

'What you don't do today will take twice as long tomorrow – and three times as long next week.'

'Doing it now' means taking action at a time when our motivation is highest and our mind remembers the segments of the task most clearly.

In our seminars which accompany *Your Pursuit of Profit*, my co-author Bill Sykes stresses the fact that most 'A' priorities take only eight minutes to complete. Research has proven that to be true.

Take away the agony

The irony of the situation is that all the time and energy spent on thinking of what we should have done is far greater than the time and energy it would take to actually do it.

If we 'do it now' the rewards look like this:

- Less guilt and stress
- More time and energy
- Rewarding sense of accomplishment and achievement
- We raise our self-esteem
- We move closer to our goals

Go for accumulated results

If we want to motivate ourselves and others, we can do what Benjamin Franklin, the successful inventor and statesman, did. Each day of the week, he focused on a different area of improvement. Then he repeated the cycle.

You have seven processes in these chapters for seven days of the week. Why not use each day to glance at the process and take some step, large or small, towards it?

A small step every day gives us enormous accumulated results. As one man said about his own life: 'I'm 36 now and it will take me four years to finish my degree while I continue working. But the way I see it is this. In four years I'll be 40 whether or not I have the degree.'

Results do not come about by one enormous effort. They come about by accumulated actions. Think about what you have always wanted to achieve. It's there for you. You need only carve out a path.

You have my support and greatest good wishes. Whatever you want must be right for you. After all, it was your mind which created it, no one else's.

Let us know what you used and the results you achieved so that we can report it to our readers and motivate our seminar attendees.

Also, let us know if you want information about our seminars. You can contact us at 20 Station Road, West Drayton, Middx, UB7-7BY, Tel 01895-431-471 or E-Mail ChristineHarvey@Compuserve.com

We look forward to hearing and reporting your progress.

Motivation Action Sheet

Use the action section below to enhance your own techniques and achievements.

Ideas for development:

1 Reach your goals by distinguishing between urgent and important.

2 Don't confuse opportunity with objective.

3 Remember that life is like a smorgasbord; choose your options carefully.

4 Don't settle for small rewards.

5 Go for accumulated results.

6 Do it now.

7 Other points as they relate to you (complete according to your needs).

Answers
- Of the above ideas, which one is likely to yield the best results for you?
- What percentage performance increase could realistically be expected?
- How long would it take:
  - to develop the idea?
  - to get results?
- Who would have to be involved?
- What date should you start?
- What is the first step you should take?

During the week, we have covered methods for motivation which bring immediate results.

The morale building process (Sunday)

- Positivity
- Gratitude
- Self-worth
- Realisation about motivation

The power to change (Monday)

- Reverse 'limitation' thinking
- The management application

The confidence building process (Tuesday)

- The process
- The self-esteem application
- The employee confidence building application
- Finding the positive side of life

The three part reinforcement process (Wednesday)

- The process
- The employee application
- The loyalty application
- The negative type

- The volunteer application
- The boss application
- The spouse application

The dolphin process (Thursday)

- The employee application
- Self-application

The anti-procrastination process (Friday)

- Make it look routine
- Sweep away all unknowns
- Push the starter button

The goal focus process (Saturday)

- Urgent versus important
- Do it now

To enquire about motivating your group with Christine Harvey as your professional speaker, contact:

Christine Harvey
Intrinsic Marketing Administrative Center
20 Station Road
West Drayton
Middlesex
UB7 7BY

Tel: 01895-431-471
Fax: 01895-422-565
E-Mail: ChristineHarvey@Compuserve.com